Critical Challenges for Primary Students

This series is one of a number of initiatives organized under the auspices of *TC² — The Critical Thinking Cooperative*. *TC²* is a partnership of British Columbia school districts, faculties of education, teacher professional associations, and other educational organizations. The aim of the cooperative is to promote critical thinking through partner-sponsored professional development, resource development and research activities. *TC²* functions as a clearinghouse and support network to promote critical thinking from primary to post-secondary education.

For more information about *TC²* contact:

LeRoi Daniels
The Critical Thinking Cooperative
c/o Richmond School District
7811 Granville Avenue
Richmond, British Columbia V6Y 3E3
Phone: (604) 732-1907   Fax: (604) 732-1957
e-mail: leroi.daniels@ubc.ca

Critical Challenges Across the Curriculum Series

Critical Challenges for Primary Students

Tami McDiarmid

Rita Manzo

Trish Musselle

The Critical
Thinking
Cooperative

Field Programs
Faculty of Education
Simon Fraser University

Series published by

The Critical Thinking Cooperative
c/o Richmond School District
7811 Granville Avenue
Richmond, British Columbia V6Y 3E3

Series produced by

Field Programs
Faculty of Education
Simon Fraser University
Burnaby, British Columbia, V5A 1S6

Design and Production: Lenore Ogilvy
Project Coordination: Patricia Holborn

Cover Design: Dynamic Desktop

Series distributed by

Pacific Educational Press
Faculty of Education
University of British Columbia
Vancouver, British Columbia, V6T 1Z4
Telephone: (604) 822-5385
Facsimile: (604) 822-6603
e-mail: cedwards@interchange.ubc.ca

CANADIAN CATALOGUING IN PUBLICATION DATA

McDiarmid, Tami Deanne, 1960-
        Critical challenges for primary students

(Critical challenges across the curriculum, ISSN 1205-0730 ; 2)
Co-published by the Critical Thinking Cooperative.
Includes biographical references.
ISBN 0-86491-147-5

1. Critical thinking—Study and teaching (Primary) I. Manzo,
Rita, 1955- II. Musselle, Patricia Lynne, 1968- III. Case,
Roland, 1951- IV. Daniels, LeRoi, 1930- V. Schwartz, Phyllis
B. (Phyllis Benna) VI. Simon Fraser University. Faculty of
Education. Field Relations and Teacher In-Service Education
VII. Critical Thinking Cooperative VIII. Title. IX. Series.

LB1590.3.M34 1996   372.13   C96-910574-6

Contents

Foreword

Critical Challenges Across the Curriculum is an ongoing series of teacher resources focussed on infusing critical thinking into every school subject. Two features distinguish this series from many other publications on critical thinking—our *curriculum embedded* approach and our emphasis on *teaching the intellectual tools.*

Our approach is to embed critical thinking by presenting focussed questions or tasks that invite critical student reflection about the content of the curriculum. We do not support the view of critical thinking as a set of generic skills or processes that can be developed independent of content and context. Nor do we believe that critical thinking can adequately be addressed as an add-on to the curriculum. Rather, if it is to take a central place in the classroom, critical thinking must be seen as a way of teaching the content of the curriculum. Teachers can help students understand the subject matter, as opposed to merely recall it, by providing continuing opportunities for thoughtful analysis of issues or problems that are central to the subject matter.

The second distinguishing feature of this series is our emphasis on systematically teaching the intellectual tools for critical thinking. Much of the frustration teachers experience when attempting to engage students in thinking critically stems from students' lack of the required concepts, attitudes, knowledge, criteria or strategies—in short, they lack the tools needed to do a competent job. It is often assumed that the mere provision of invitations to think will improve students' reflective competence. We believe that constructing a thoughtful response is like building a house, in that it is impossible to do a competent job in either case unless one has the necessary tools. For this reason, each critical thinking challenge in the series includes a list of the tools needed to respond competently and, more importantly, activities suggesting how these tools may be taught.

We hope that teachers will find these resources of use in increasing and improving the teaching of critical thinking in their subject areas.

Roland Case & LeRoi Daniels

Series Editors

Preface and Acknowledgments

As many of our colleagues have known for years, young children can think for themselves and think critically provided they are given appropriate conditions and direction. We have personally used each of the critical challenges in this resource in our own primary classrooms.

We would like to thank the following educators for their support:

Laurie Anderson	Vancouver School District
Mark Frein	University of British Columbia
Valerie Overgaard	Vancouver School District
Phyllis Schwartz	Vancouver School District
Bev Price	Vancouver School District

Development of this resource was co-sponsored by The Vancouver School District.

Tami McDiarmid, Rita Manzo & Trish Musselle

Guide to the Lesson Format

Each of the critical challenges in this resource has the following components.

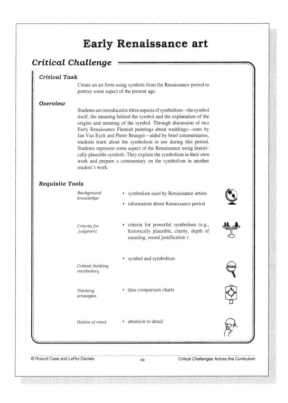

The **critical challenge** opens with a **critical question** or **critical task** that students will be asked to address.

An **overview** describes the focus of the lesson and the main activities that students will undertake.

Requisite tools provides an inventory of the specific intellectual resources that students will need to use in competently addressing the critical challenge.

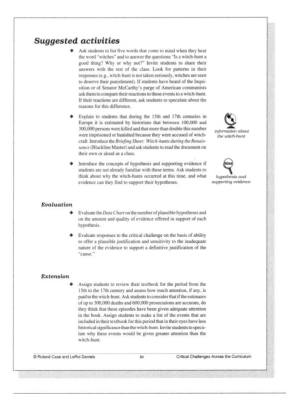

The body of the lesson is found under **suggested activities** which indicate how the critical challenge may be introduced and how the requisite tools may be taught. **Icons** in the side panel point out which specific tool is being addressed. Also provided in **evaluation** are assessment criteria and procedures, and in **extension** are found ideas for further exploration or broader application of key ideas found in the lesson. **References** are provided whenever published resources are referred to in the lesson plan.

Introduction to Critical Thinking

Understanding Critical Thinking

There are many conceptions or accounts of what is involved in thinking critically. The model described here is more fully explained in two articles in the *Journal of Curriculum Studies* entitled "Common Misconceptions of Critical Thinking" and "A Conception of Critical Thinking" by Sharon Bailin, Roland Case, Jerrold Coombs and LeRoi Daniels. For reasons explained below, we propose the following definition:

> *Critical thinking involves thinking through problematic situations about what to believe or how to act where the thinker makes reasoned judgments that embody the qualities of a competent thinker.*

A person is attempting to think critically when she thoughtfully seeks to judge what would be sensible or reasonable to believe or do in a given situation. The need to reach reasoned judgments may arise in countless kinds of problematic situations such as trying to understand a passage in a text, trying to improve an artistic performance, making effective use of a piece of equipment, or deciding how to act in a delicate social situation. What makes these situations problematic is that there is some doubt as to the most appropriate option.

Critical thinking is sometimes contrasted with problem solving, decision making, issue analysis and inquiry. We see these latter terms for rational deliberation as occasions for critical thinking. In all these situations, we need to think critically about the options. There is limited value in reaching solutions or making choices that are not sensible or reasonable. Thus, the term critical thinking draws attention to the quality of thinking required to competently pose and solve problems, reach sound decisions, identify and resolve issues, plan and conduct thoughtful inquiries and so on. In other words, thinking critically is a way of carrying out these thinking tasks just as being careful is a way of walking down the stairs. Thinking critically is not a unique *type* of thinking that is different from other types of thinking, rather it refers to the *quality* of thinking. The association of critical thinking with being negative or judgmental is misleading, since the reference to critical is to distinguish it from uncritical thinking—thinking that accepts conclusions at face value without any assessment of their merits or bases. It is more fruitful to interpret critical in the sense of critique—looking at the merits and shortcomings of alternatives in order to arrive at a reasoned judgment.

Our focus on the quality of thinking does not imply that students must arrive at a preconceived right answer, rather we look to see that their responses exhibit the qualities that characterize good thinking in a given situation. For example, students' responses to a request to cooperatively plan a field trip through group discussion may be judged in light of the accuracy and adequacy of information, how seriously students considered the ideas of others, willingness to express their own ideas, and respect for the ideas of those with whom they disagree. These are all qualities that a competent thinker would exhibit. Similarly, a critically thoughtful response to a newspaper editorial would likely include the following characteristics: sensitivity to any bias on the part of the writer, adequate consideration of alternative points of view, attention to the clarity of definition of key concepts, and assessment of evidence offered in support of the writer's position. We believe that emphasis on qualities that student responses should exhibit focuses teachers' attention on the crucial dimension in promoting and assessing students' competence in thinking critically. The challenge for teachers is to adopt practices that will effectively promote these qualities in their students.

Promoting Critical Thinking

To help students improve as critical thinkers, we propose a four-pronged approach:

- build a *community of thinkers* within the school and classroom;

- infuse opportunities for critical thinking—what we call *critical challenges*—throughout the curriculum;

- develop the *intellectual tools* that will enable students to become competent critical thinkers;

- on a continuing basis *assess students' competence* in using the intellectual tools to think through critical challenges.

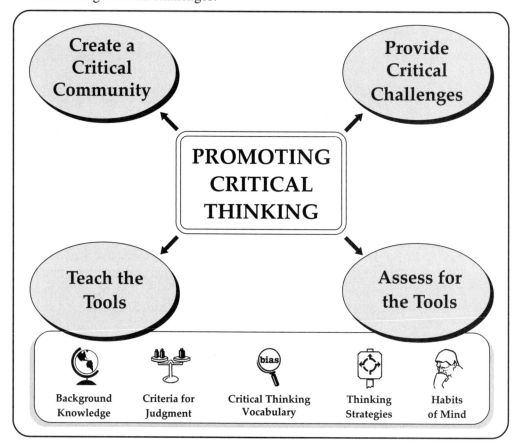

Building a community of thinkers

It is essential to infuse the expectations and opportunities to think critically throughout students' school lives. Developing supportive school and classroom communities where reflective inquiry is valued may be the most important factor in nurturing critical thinking. Many of the tools of critical thinking will not be mastered by students unless their use is reinforced on an ongoing basis. As well, the image of the thinker as a solitary figure is misleading. No one person can perfectly embody all the desired attributes—we must learn to rely on others to complement our own thoughts. Students will not learn how to be contributors to, and beneficiaries of, a community of thinkers unless they become members in that kind of community. There are many routines and norms that teachers can adopt to create this sense of community:

- As a matter of course, questions and assignments should have built-in expectations to think through, and not merely recall, what is being learned.

- Ongoing opportunities to engage in critical and cooperative dialogue—to confer, inquire, debate and critique—are key to creating a community of thinkers.

- Self- and peer-evaluation are excellent ways of involving students in thinking critically about their own work.

- Teacher modelling of good critical thinking practices is important. Students are more likely to learn to act in desired ways if they see teachers making every effort to be open-minded, to seek clarification where needed, to avoid reaching conclusions based on inadequate evidence, and so on. Opportunities to see their teachers as co-investigators, and not solely as resident experts, may send important messages to students about the need to think critically.

Infusing critical challenges throughout the curriculum

Critical thinking is always in response to a problematic situation, where judgment among alternatives is required. If students are to improve in their ability to think critically, they must have numerous opportunities to engage and think through problematic situations. We label as *critical challenges* those problematic situations which are deliberately presented to students for consideration.

Four questions should guide the choice of critical challenges.

- *Does the question or task require judgment?* Critical thinking occurs only in the context of a problematic situation. If an answer is simply there, waiting to be found, or if any and all answers are acceptable then there is no invitation to think critically. A question or task is a critical challenge only if it invites students to assess the reasonableness of plausible options or alternative conclusions; in short, the task must require more than retrieval of information, rote application of a strategy, uninformed guessing or mere assertion of a preference.

- *Will the challenge be meaningful to students?* We enhance our efforts to promote critical thinking if students find the questions interesting. Trivial, decontextualized mental exercises often alienate or bore students. It is important to frame challenges that are likely to engage students in tackling critical questions and tasks that they will find meaningful.

- *Does the challenge address key aspects of the subject matter?* If we are to make time for critical thinking the focus must be on matters that are at the heart of the curriculum—and not peripheral to it. As well, students are more likely to learn the content of the curriculum if they are invited to think critically about issues embedded in the subject matter.

- *Do students have the tools or can they reasonably acquire the tools needed to competently address the challenge?* Students are more likely to succeed if they possess the tools to deal with the challenge before them. Provision must be made to support students in acquiring the essential tools needed to competently meet the critical challenge. For this reason, challenges should be sufficiently focussed so that students are not overwhelmed by the enormity or complexity of the task.

Developing intellectual tools for thinking critically

The key to helping students develop as critical thinkers is to nurture competent use of five types of tools of thinking. These categories of tools are *background knowledge, criteria for judgment, critical thinking vocabulary, thinking strategies* and *habits of mind.*

Background Knowledge

—the information about a topic required for thoughtful reflection

Students cannot think deeply about a topic if they know little about it. Two questions to ask in developing this tool:

- What background information do students need for them to make a well-informed judgment on the matter before them?
- How can students be assisted in acquiring this information in a meaningful matter?

Criteria for Judgment

—the considerations or grounds for deciding which of the alternatives is the most sensible or appropriate

Critical thinking is essentially a matter of judging which alternative is sensible or reasonable. All judgments are based on criteria of some sort or other. Students need help in thinking carefully about the criteria to use when judging various alternatives.

- Is my estimate *accurate*?
- Is the interpretation *plausible?*
- Is the conclusion *fair* to all?
- Is my proposal *feasible*?

Critical Thinking Vocabulary

—the range of concepts and distinctions that are helpful when thinking critically

Students require the vocabulary or concepts that permit them to make important distinctions among the different issues and thinking tasks facing them. These include the following:

- inference and direct observation;
- generalization and over generalization;
- premise and conclusion;
- bias and point of view.

Thinking Strategies

—the repertoire of heuristics, organizing devices, models and algorithms that may be useful when thinking through a critical thinking problem

Although critical thinking is never simply a matter of following certain procedures or steps, numerous strategies are useful for guiding one's performance when thinking critically:

- *Making decisions:* Are there models or procedures to guide students through the factors they should consider (e.g., a framework for issue analysis or problem solving)?
- *Organizing information:* Would a graphic organizer (e.g., webbing diagrams, Venn diagrams, "pro and con" charts) be useful in representing what a student knows about the issue?
- *Role taking:* Before deciding on an action that affects others, should students put themselves in the others' positions and imagine their feelings?

Habits of Mind

—the values and attitudes of a careful and conscientious thinker

Being able to apply criteria and use strategies is of little value unless students also have the habits of mind of a thoughtful person. These include:

- *Open-minded:* Are students willing to consider evidence opposing their view and to revise their view should the evidence warrant it?
- *Fair-minded:* Are students willing to give impartial consideration to alternative points of view and not simply impose their preference?
- *Independent-minded:* Are students willing to stand up for their firmly held beliefs?
- *Inquiring or "critical" attitude:* Are students inclined to question the clarity of and support for claims and to seek justified beliefs and values?

Assessing for the tools

Assessment is an important complement to the teaching of the tools of critical thinking. As suggested by the familiar adages "What is counted counts" and "Testing drives the curriculum," evaluation has important implications for what students consider important and ultimately what students learn. Evaluations that focus exclusively on recall of information or never consider habits of mind fail to assess, and possibly discourage, student growth in critical reflection.

A key challenge in assessing critical thinking is deciding what to look for in a student's answer. If there is no single correct response, we may well ask: "On what basis, then, can we reliably assess students?" The qualities that we would expect to see exhibited in a successful response should provide the basis for our assessments. In the case of critical thinking, this means we would want to see whether or not students exhibited the qualities of a competent thinker. Thus, the intellectual resources or tools for critical thinking become the criteria for assessing students' work. More specifically, as students respond (orally, in writing, visually, etc.) to a critical challenge we should look for indications of the extent to which their comments or products reveal appropriate use of the desired tools. In other words, has the student:

- provided adequate and accurate information?
- satisfied relevant criteria for judgment?
- revealed understanding of important vocabulary?
- made effective use of appropriate thinking strategies?
- demonstrated the desired habits of mind?

The following example suggests each of the five types of critical thinking tools and specific assessment criteria that might be used in assessing evidence of critical thinking in an argumentative essay and an artistic work.

Type of criteria for assessment	Evidence of critical thinking in a persuasive essay	Evidence of critical thinking in an artistic work
Background Knowledge	• cited accurate information.	• revealed knowledge of the mechanics of the medium.
Criteria for Judgment	• provided ample evidence; • arranged arguments in logical sequence.	• work was imaginative; • work was clear and forceful.
Critical Thinking Vocabulary	• correctly distinguished "arguments" from "counter arguments."	• represented "point of view."
Thinking Strategies	• used appropriate strategies for persuasive writing.	• employed suitable rehearsal/preparation strategies.
Habits of Mind	• demonstrated an openness to alternative perspectives; • refrained from forming firm opinions where the evidence was inconclusive.	• was open to constructive criticism; • demonstrated a commitment to high quality; • demonstrated a willingness to take risks with the medium.

Peer- and self-assessment are especially effective means of encouraging critical thinking since the assessment of an assignment is a synonym for thinking critically about the assignment. The box below contains statements about several thinking strategies and habits of mind that students might consider as they self-assess their thoughtfulness as independent learners.

Self-assessment questions	Implied criteria for assessment
I thought about what I was expected to do before I started.	*Thinking Strategy:* before beginning, get clear about expectations
I asked for help whenever I needed it.	*Thinking Strategy:* ask for help
I stayed "on-task" until all my work was finished.	*Habit of Mind:* intellectual work ethic
I tried my best.	*Habit of Mind:* intellectual work ethic

Overview of Critical Challenges

Community / environment

Building structures	Students learn some principles of construction and about using criteria to judge performance. Students build different structures that satisfy specific criteria set by the teacher. They are also asked to explain why their structures may meet or fail to meet one of the criteria. As an extension, students generate their own criteria and attempt to build a structure that satisfies these criteria.
A picture is worth a thousand words	Students are asked to take a photograph which depicts a previously chosen feature or quality of their community (e.g., friendly, dangerous, fun). Other students try to match the quality with the photograph and explain why the photograph reflects this quality.
Design a community	After extensive study of communities, students brainstorm the qualities to be found in a good community and the services and facilities that best provide for these qualities. Students then design an ideal community using materials of their choice. Students are to explain the qualities and services reflected in their plan.
Insect habitat	After observing various insects in the classroom and the natural environment, and after studying about them in films and books, students work together to identify the features of a desirable insect habitat. Students use the criteria they identify to design a habitat for an insect of their choice.
Problem in a picture? Solve it	Based on a picture card from the *Second Step* series, students explore a situation depicted in a photograph involving a child feeling unwelcome. After brainstorming possible solutions, students select and give reasons for the best solution based on criteria they have generated. Students are encouraged to see that problems can be addressed in several ways but that some solutions are better than others.

Human nature

The wolf's "real" character	Students consider a traditional version of the "The Three Little Pigs" and then examine *The True Story of the Three Little Pigs,* by Jon Scieszka. In this non-traditional version, the wolf claims to have been unfairly characterized as the bad guy. Students are encouraged to find evidence in the text to support their own conclusion about the wolf's real character. They are asked to see through the obvious rationalization offered by the wolf.
Predicting a winner	Based on the story *The Boxing Champion,* by Roch Carrier, students consider whether or not the author is likely to win his boxing match. Part way through the story students use clues in the text to predict the outcome of the story and justify their predictions. Because the author paints an unrealistic portrait of his prospects, students must infer why he may not win his bout.
It's so nice to have a wolf around the house	Based on the book/video *It's So Nice To Have a Wolf Around the House* students consider whether the wolf, Cuthbert Q. Devine, is a hero or a scoundrel. Students are encouraged to provide evidence for both conclusions and to be open to the possibility that things may not be as they first appear.

Moral dilemmas

The discovery	In the story *Jack and the Meanstalk,* by Brian and Rebecca Wildsmith, Professor Jack discovers a way of dramatically increasing the size of plants. Students brainstorm possible consequences of this discovery and weigh the pros and cons before deciding whether or not Professor Jack's secret should be shared with the rest of the world.
Rumpelstiltskin and the conditions for kindness	Students consider when it is that they have a responsibility to help others in need and when they do not. They then view the film *Rumpelstiltskin,* listen to the story and decide if Rumpelstiltskin was right in demanding something from the miller's daughter in exchange for saving her life.
Making a difference	Students are invited to consider what they can do to make a lasting difference in someone else's life. Hopefully, students will increase awareness of their own good fortune and see that there are always others who are worse off. The inspiration for the challenge is the picture book *A Handful of Seeds,* by Monica Hughes, which tells of a girl in Latin America who helps a group of street kids. Also instructive is the novel *Wingman,* by Daniel Manus Pickwater, about a family insulted by being made to feel poor.

Moral dilemmas (continued)

Right or wrong?	The stealing of a trumpet in E.B. White's novel *The Trumpet of the Swan* is used to focus discussion on when, if ever, it is justifiable to do something that is wrong. In this story the parent of a young swan steals a trumpet to provide the young voiceless swan with a way to communicate. Other stories which raise a similar dilemma may be used—for example, "Robin Hood" (stealing from the rich to give to the poor) or "Jack and the Beanstalk" (stealing a hen to provide food).

Me and my family

My own character and personality traits	Students are asked to judge what kinds of character or personality traits are positive. Using that knowledge, students choose three positive traits which best fit themselves. Other students then try to guess which traits fit which students, and to provide evidence to support their guess.
Powerful memories	The story *Wilfred Gordon McDonald Partridge,* by Mem Fox, explains how an elderly woman is aided in regaining her lost memory by a little boy who brings things that trigger her memory. This story is used to stimulate students into thinking of their most powerful memory and what makes it so powerful.
Assigning household tasks	Students imagine they are parents. They are asked to divide up four household chores in their own homes in a fair and effective manner.
The trouble with Mama	In the story *Monster Mama,* by Liz Rosenberg, Patrick Edward is a typical seven-year old, but his mother is a Monster. Students consider the question "What makes a good parent?" before reading the story. Students then decide if Patrick Edward's mother is a good parent and justify their answer based on criteria they generate and on evidence from the story.

Teaching and learning from others

Powerful questions	In preparation for a visit by a classroom guest, students brainstorm criteria for a *powerful* question. In pairs, students use the criteria to assess questions that they have generated individually. Each student selects a powerful question to ask of the guest.
Teaching the value of money	Students design an activity to determine whether or not other students have met a curricular outcome dealing with money—for example, that students can recognize the value of coins and give change for $1.00. The planned activity should meet criteria agreed to by the class.
Create a trick	Using some simple materials, students create magic tricks. The class discusses what makes a magic trick successful, including the idea of illusion.

Building structures

Critical Challenge

Critical Task

Build a structure that meets the specified criteria.

Overview

Students learn about some principles of construction and about using criteria to judge performance. Students build different structures that satisfy specific criteria set by the teacher. They are also asked to explain why their structures may meet or fail to met one of the criteria. As an extension, students generate their own criteria and attempt to build a structure that satisfies these criteria.

Requisite Tools

Background knowledge	• basic principles of construction	
Criteria for judgment	• specified criteria for the structure (e.g., rigidity, strength, stability)	
Critical thinking vocabulary	• hypothesis and hypothesis testing • criteria	
Thinking strategies		
Habits of mind	• attention to detail	

Suggested Activities

◆ Set up the following construction materials for each pair of students:

- toothpicks (50 per pair)

- plasticine (approximately 1/2 cup per pair)

- heavy manila tag (for reinforcement).

◆ Allow students in pairs time to explore and play with the plasticine and toothpicks. Meet to discuss with pairs of students what they discovered about the properties of those materials: "What did you notice? Why do you think that it was this way?"

principles of construction

◆ Ask students to make use of what they found out about the materials, to construct either a box-like shape or a pyramid that is rigid (i.e., does not wobble). Ask one half of the class to construct a rectangle and the other half to construct a pyramid. Allow students sufficient time to work and investigate, then call them back into a large group and discuss their findings.

◆ Explain to students that the two conditions—a particular shape (either a pyramid or a rectangle) and a specific design feature (no wobble)—are referred to as "criteria." Explain that criteria refer to the features that we use for judging whether something meets the desired requirements. Ask students to check whether or not their structures met the two criteria.

criteria

◆ Ask students to make the rigid, strong shape that they did not make. (If they made the pyramid, then try to make the box. If they made the box, then make the pyramid.) Discuss again in the large group.

◆ Present the challenge by explaining to students that the next structure they will be building must meet three criteria:

- must be a specific *height*   7 centimeters

- must *support a given weight*   200 grams

- must be constructed *within a materials allowance*   using fewer than 50 toothpicks, fewer than 10 manila tags, and use plasticine no larger than the size of green peas.

criteria for the structure

◆ To help students determine if their structure meets these criteria, provide each pair with the following:

- • ruler (for measuring height)

- • small book or other weight of about 200 grams (to be used to test supporting weight)

- • green pea (to judge size of plasticine).

◆ Allow students sufficient time to create their structures, and encourage them to pay close attention to whether or not they have met the three criteria.

attention to detail

◆ If their structures collapse, ask students to generate a hypothesis to explain why, and then test their hypothesis so as to make their structure stronger. If their initial structure successfully supports the weight, ask students to generate a hypothesis about why it did so.

hypothesis and hypothesis testing

◆ Have students share their structures and their hypotheses with the whole class.

Evaluation

◆ Evaluate the activity by determining if students can assess their structure against the criteria by demonstrating that it is the specified height, supports the specified weight, and is within the materials allowance.

◆ Assess whether students try to generate and test their hypotheses.

Extension

◆ Follow up the lesson by reading the story *Tar Beach*, by Faith Ringgold, or watch the video *Rainbow*.

◆ Ask students to create their own challenges using the same materials by setting different criteria for height, weight and materials allowance (e.g., How many supplies do they think that they might need?). Invite students to consider how they will test its strength, its height, and whether they were under or over their projected materials allowance.

References

Tar Beach by Faith Ringgold (Crown Publishers, New York, 1991).

Rainbow (Video).

A picture is worth a thousand words

Critical Challenge

Critical Task

Working in pairs, take a photograph within school grounds (or in the neighbouring community) that captures the particular quality of the community that you have been assigned.

Overview

Students are asked to take a photograph which depicts a previously chosen feature or quality of their community (e.g., friendly, dangerous, fun). Other students try to match the quality with the photograph and explain why the photograph reflects this quality.

Requisite Tools

Background knowledge	• knowledge of community • how to use a camera	
Criteria for judgment	• features of a good picture (e.g., fits a caption, has sufficient detail)	
Critical thinking vocabulary		
Thinking strategies		
Habits of mind		

Suggested Activities

◆ Ask students to brainstorm words (adjectives and adverbs) that describe their community environment (e.g., friendly, happy, fun, dirty).

Knowledge of community

◆ Write each word (or phrase) on a separate index card and place the cards in a large envelope. These words are now captions. Students in pairs choose a card from the envelope without looking. Each pair of students keeps the card (with caption) they picked to themselves.

◆ Introduce the critical task to the class:

> Working in pairs, take a photograph within school grounds (or in the neighbouring community) that captures the particular quality of the community that you have been assigned.

◆ Before sending students out, discuss the criteria of a good picture. This may be done by sharing several photographs of varying quality with the class and asking them to identify features that they note. Three criteria are particularly key for this activity:

features of good photographs

- the image is large enough to be recognizable

- there are sufficient details to send a message

- the image matches the caption.

◆ If students are unfamiliar with the use of cameras, provide instructions and a few tips for taking good photographs. Cameras that produce the photograph immediately are most appropriate for this activity.

use of a camera

◆ When students return to class, tape their captions and photographs in separate groups on a board. Each pair takes a turn pointing to their picture (without revealing which is their caption) while other members of the class guess which caption belongs with the picture and explain why they think it fits.

◆ The class is allowed three guesses for each picture. If a guess is correct or after three failed guesses, the pair explains to the class what caption their picture represents and gives their reason for taking this picture to represent their caption.

Evaluation

◆ Assess how well each photograph fits the identified criteria for a good picture. Are students able to give reasons for choosing a picture to go with a particular caption?

Extension

◆ Discuss with the class if any of the photographs changed how students viewed their community.

◆ Look for and discuss similarities and differences among the pictures.

◆ Invite students to create new captions for the pictures.

◆ Invite students to locate and assemble magazine photographs that depict the original captions of the community to create a neighbourhood montage.

Design a community

Critical Challenge

Critical Task

Design an ideal community.

Overview

After extensive study of communities, students brainstorm the qualities to be found in a good community and the services and facilities that best provide for these qualities. Students then design an ideal community using materials of their choice. Students are to explain how the desired qualities are reflected in the facilities and services in their plan.

Requisite Tools

Background knowledge	• knowledge of the workings of a city or other community	
Criteria for judgment	• qualities and services of a good community (e.g., health, traffic flow, safety)	
Critical thinking vocabulary		
Thinking strategies	• T-chart	
Habits of mind		

Suggested Activities

◆ This critical task is best used at the end of a unit on the village, town or city as a community. It is expected that students have benefited from direct experiences with their own community (e.g., walks around their community, tours of shops, visits from local people) and class discussions, books and videos about the idea of city as a community.

workings of a city

◆ Introduce students to two ideas: (1) the qualities or criteria of a good community and (2) the services or facilities that provide or support these qualities. Suggest, for example, that a good community is one in which the citizens are healthy; in other words, "healthy people" is a quality of a good community. Ask students to suggest some of the services or facilities within a community that contribute to our health (e.g., hospitals, doctors, garbage collection).

◆ On poster paper, create a T-chart using the headings listed below. To illustrate how the chart works, write down the words "healthy people" in the left-hand column and record the facilities and services that students generated in the right-hand column.

T-chart

Qualities of a good community	Services and facilities that support these qualities
• *healthy people*	• *hospitals* • *doctors* • *garbage collection*

◆ As a whole class, have students brainstorm other qualities of a good community and suggest the services and facilities that promote or support these qualities. Depending on the class, the teacher may suggest very sophisticated qualities (e.g., traffic flow, mental health) and "alternative" services and facilities (e.g., solar housing, electric cars). Keep the chart in a prominent place so that additional ideas can be added as students progress through the critical challenge.

qualities and services of a good community

◆ Present the critical task:

Design an ideal community.

Suggest to students that they have an opportunity to design their ideal community. They are to identify the qualities that they think are important and to decide how and in what way these qualities can be realized—i.e., what services and facilities they need in their community.

◆ Allow students to decide how they wish to present the design of their community—they may want to consider lego, big blocks, junk art, drawing, plasticine, and so on. The work may be done in small groups or individually.

◆ As students are working on their designs, encourage them to consider the qualities that were generated by the class and to think about how best to provide for the qualities they desire. Encourage students to consult books and other references for ideas on how other communities have provided for essential and desirable services and facilities.

◆ After completing their design, students are to explain to the class what qualities they have built into their community and what services and facilities support these qualities.

Evaluation

◆ Assess each design by considering the extent to which students have included essential qualities of a good community and that their proposed facilities or services are thoughtful ways of meeting these requirements. (Have students considered the cause and effect relationship between the criteria and the services in their design? Do students have reasons for their choice of location for services?)

◆ You may also wish to assess also the degree of imagination both in the design of the community and in the use of medium to represent the design.

Extension

◆ Invite the class as a whole to assess each design to see which proposals seem to meet the qualities identified by the class.

◆ Invite students to find ways to join together their communities. How would such expansion affect their communities? What new things must they think of? Talk about suburbs, how they are formed and why they occur.

Insect habitat

Critical Challenge

Critical Task

Design a desirable habitat for an insect of your choice.

Overview

After observing various insects in the classroom and the natural environment, and after studying about them in films and books, students work together to identify the features of a desirable insect habitat. Students use the criteria they identify to design a habitat for an insect of their choice.

Requisite Tools

Background knowledge	• habitat needs of various insects	
Criteria for judgment	• features of a good habitat for a particular insect	
Critical thinking vocabulary		
Thinking strategies	• information webbing	
Habits of mind	• inquiring or critical attitude	

Suggested Activities

◆ Ask students what they know about habitats. Show the short video *In Your Backyard*, by David Suzuki.

needs of various insects

◆ In a large group, create a web of the ideas from the video on habitats. Explain that the web is a strategy for recording information, and that students will be asked to expand upon the web as they learn more about habitats.

webbing

◆ Read *The Magic School Bus Hops Home* by Patricia Relf and others. Use this book to add to the web of ideas about the features of a habitat.

◆ Involve the class in some form of direct observation of insects. To do this they may collect and observe: how snails grow, study worms in a worm compost, raise butterflies from the larval stage, or be taken on a nature walk. (One strategy for focussing attention while on a nature walk is to place a hoola hoop on the ground in front of a small group of students and have them watch carefully the goings-on for two minutes.) After their direct observation opportunities, as a group, add to the web of habitat ideas.

needs of various insects

◆ Refer to the information web as a means of helping the class develop a set of criteria for a good habitat. Record students' ideas (e.g., supply of water, place to hide, food source) on a class chart.

features of a habitat

◆ After considerable background knowledge has been developed, read *The Salamander Room* by Anne Mazer, a story about a boy who created a habitat for his salamander. Ask students if they would like to make a home for an insect. If students are interested ask them to consider what would be the desirable features of this habitat.

◆ Present the critical task to the class:

Design a habitat for an insect of your choice.

◆ After completing their designs, ask students to share and critically discuss each others' designs in light of the criteria of a good habitat.

Evaluation

◆ While students are creating their design, observe to see if they exhibit an inquiring and critical attitude for the task:

  • Do students ask questions about their insects and their habitats?

  • Do they attempt to find out more about their insects and its habitat needs?

  • Do students consider and seriously try to meet the criteria when making their design choices?

  • Also consider how well the designs reflect the criteria that the class set for a good habitat. Do other students recognize when a design meets the established criteria?

inquiring or critical attitude

Extension

◆ As a follow-up, students could talk or write about their habitats and their experience in designing the habitats. They could propose ways of keeping those habitats safe and this could lead to a discussion on our environment and how they could help to keep it a safe and healthy place. Discuss what would happen if we were to take away parts of the habitat. How would this change the insect or the environment has a whole?

◆ The class may decide to select a few insects as class pets for a short while and actually construct a few of the designs that they thought would best suit their pet insects.

References

In Your Backyard (video) by David Suzuki.

The Salamander Room by Anne Mazer (Alfred A. Knopf, New York, 1991).

The Magic School Bus Hops Home by Patricia Relf, Joanna Cole, and Nancy W. Stevenson (Scholastic Publications, New York, 1991).

Problem in a picture?
Solve it

Critical Challenge

Critical Question

Which of the suggested solutions to the problem situation depicted in the photograph best reflects the qualities of a friendly person?

Overview

Based on a picture card from the *Second Step* series, students explore a situation depicted in a photograph involving a child feeling unwelcome. After brainstorming possible solutions, students select and give reasons for the best solution based on criteria they have generated. Students are encouraged to see that problems can be addressed in several ways but that some solutions are better than others.

Requisite Tools

Background knowledge	• knowledge of ways of helping others	
Criteria for judgment	• qualities of a friendly person	
Critical thinking vocabulary		
Thinking strategies	• information chart • role play of solutions	
Habits of mind	• empathy	

Suggested Activities

◆ Select a picture from the *Second Step* series that raises the question of making fellow students feel welcome in a group.

◆ Ask students to state what they notice, what feelings the picture brings out, what the picture make them think of. Encourage students to think how they would feel if they were one of the children in the picture.

empathy

◆ In small groups ask students to share their responses and discuss possible solutions to the situation in the photograph.

◆ Have each group share one solution with the entire class. Record these solutions.

ways of helping others

◆ Ask the class to think of the qualities of a friendly person—for example, doing kind things for people, showing others that you like them, caring about others.

qualities of a friendly person

◆ Set up a chart, such as the one shown below, with three columns. Invite students to brainstorm the qualities of a friendly person and the actions that do and do not exhibit these qualities.

information chart

Recognizing friendly people		
Qualities of a friendly person	Actions that show friendly qualities	Actions that do NOT show friendly qualities
• showing that you like people	• smiles at people	• says mean things to people

◆ Return to the solutions generated by the class to the problem depicted in the photograph and present the critical question:

Which of the suggested solutions to the problem situation depicted in the photograph best reflects the qualities of a friendly person?

◆ Ask the students to match the suggested solutions against the qualities in the chart. To help students make up their minds, have different groups role play the situation in the picture and the varying solutions they have suggested.

role play

◆ Ask students individually to write or draw a response to the picture (or to a situation when they had a similar experience) that they think would be the most friendly solution to the problem. Students should give reasons for believing that their solution is the best by referring to the qualities of friendly person generated by the class.

Evaluation

◆ Assess how well students are able to match their solutions to the qualities of a friendly person.

Extension

◆ Introduce other cards in the *Second Set* series involving the same characters. Ask groups of students to role play various cards.

◆ Using other cards in the *Second Set* series, have students practice verbalizing the problem, and verbalizing a solution.

References

Second Step by Kathy Belland (Institute for Child Advocacy, Seattle, WA, 1989).

The wolf's "real" character

Critical Challenge

Critical Question

Is the Wolf in *The True Story of the Three Little Pigs* good or bad?

Overview

Students consider a traditional version of the "The Three Little Pigs" and then examine *The True Story of the Three Little Pigs* by Jon Scieszka. In this non-traditional version, the wolf claims to have been unfairly characterized as the bad guy. Students are encouraged to find evidence in the text to support their own conclusion about the wolf's real character. They are asked to see through the obvious rationalization offered by the wolf.

Requisite Tools

Background knowledge	• details of *The True Story of the Three Little Pigs*	
Criteria for judgment	• evidence from the text to support conclusions	
Critical thinking vocabulary	• evidence	
Thinking strategies	• recording evidence	
Habits of mind	• inquiring or critical attitude	

Suggested Activities

◆ Read aloud a traditional version of "The Three Little Pigs".

◆ In a large group record all the events from the text that provide evidence about the wolf's character. If students are unfamiliar with the term 'evidence' ask for a definition (e.g., information that help us decide what to believe) and provide them with examples (e.g., If I helped my parents tidy the house would that be evidence of me being a good worker or bad worker?).

evidence

◆ Read aloud *The True Story of the Three Little Pigs*.

details of the story

◆ In groups of three, have students consider the critical question:

> Is the Wolf in *The True Story of the Three Little Pigs* good or bad?

Ask students to decide as a group whether the Wolf in this story is good or bad. Have them identify all the evidence in the text that tells us about the Wolf's character and use pictures or words to record this evidence.

evidence from the text

◆ In a large group ask students to share their conclusions and their supporting evidence. As the discussion progresses, use a chart such as the following to record the evidence for and against taking the Wolf's version of what happened.

recording evidence

The Wolf said or did . . .	Think 'Yes' Evidence that supports the Wolf's version	Think 'No' Evidence that questions the Wolf's version

◆ After sharing the information allow students to re-think their original conclusion and whether or not they want to change their mind.

critical attitude

Evaluation

◆ In the small group activity, assess whether students are able to identify evidence that supports their conclusion. In the large group activity, assess whether students could see any inconsistency between the Wolf's statements and behaviour.

References

The True Story of the Three Little Pigs by Jon Scieszka (illustrated by Lane Smith, Viking, New York, 1989).

Predicting a winner

Critical Challenge

Critical Task

Use words or pictures to complete Roch Carrier's story, *The Boxing Champion*.

Overview

Based on the story *The Boxing Champion* by Roch Carrier students consider whether or not the author is likely to win his boxing match. Part way through the story students use clues in the text to predict the outcome of the story and to justify their predictions. Because the author paints an unrealistic portrait of his prospects, students must infer from the text why he may not win his bout.

Requisite Tools

Background knowledge	• details of Carrier's *The Boxing Champion* • some people have unrealistic pictures of themselves	
Criteria for judgment	• fits the story	
Critical thinking vocabulary	• evidence or "clues"	
Thinking strategies	• information recording chart	
Habits of mind	• inquiring or critical attitude	

Suggested Activities

◆ Read aloud *The Boxing Champion* up to the point where Roch enters the ring after his secret training ("The bell rang. I attacked like a champion.").

details of the story

◆ Ask students to consider whether they think Roch will win or not. Discuss the way a detective will look for evidence or clues to suggest what happened or what will happen. Acting as detectives, have students consider clues in the text that indicate the outcome of the boxing match.

evidence or clues

◆ Pose the critical task:

Use words or pictures to complete Roch Carrier's story *The Boxing Champion*.

Ask students to list the clues which support their conclusion.

◆ Share the different endings created by each student. Using an information recording chart like the one suggested below; have students identify as a whole class all the evidence or clues in the text to suggest why Roch may win and why he may not win.

consistency with text

Clues that Roch may win	Clues that Roch may not win

information chart

◆ Have students discuss in a small group which outcome is the most likely given the clues in the text. Encourage them to go beyond what Roch says he can do.

critical attitude

◆ Read the ending of the story, and discuss why the author led the readers to believe that things would happen differently. Ask students to consider any clues in the story that suggest Roch had an unrealistic impression of his boxing talents.

unrealistic impressions of self

Evaluation

◆ Assess whether the clues students offer are consistent with information in the story.

Extension

◆ Ask students to share a time when they may have had an unrealistic picture of themselves.

References

The Boxing Champion by Roch Carrier (illustrated by Sheldon Cohen, translated by Stella Fischman, Turdia Publications, Montreal, 1991).

It's so nice to have a wolf around the house

Critical Challenge

Critical Question

Is Cuthbert a hero or a scoundrel?

Overview

Based on the book/video *It's So Nice To Have a Wolf Around the House* students consider whether the wolf, Cuthbert Q. Devine, is a hero or a scoundrel. Students are encouraged to provide evidence for both conclusions and to be open to the possibility that things may not be as they first appear.

Requisite Tools

Background knowledge	• details of the story *It's So Nice To Have a Wolf Around the House*	
Criteria for judgment	• traits that characterize heroes and scoundrels	
Critical thinking vocabulary	• evidence and conclusion	
Thinking strategies	• T-chart	
Habits of mind	• open-minded	

Suggested Activities

♦ Introduce the book/video, *It's So Nice To Have a Wolf Around the House*. Ask students to pay particular attention to the character, Cuthbert Q. Devine.

details of the story

♦ Explain the difference between a hero and a scoundrel. Discuss how heroes and scoundrels act. Ask students to consider the critical question:

Is Cuthbert a hero or a scoundrel?

traits of hero and scoundrel

♦ In groups of three, students brainstorm evidence from the story to support both conclusions—Cuthbert as hero and as scoundrel. In a large group record all the events from the text that provide evidence about the wolf's character. If students are unfamiliar with the term 'evidence' ask for a definition (e.g., information that help us decide what to believe) and provide them with examples (e.g., If I helped my parents tidy the house would that be evidence of me being a good worker or bad worker?). Explain that a *conclusion* is the answer reached after all the evidence has been considered.

evidence and conclusion

♦ Using pictures or words, students record their ideas on a T-chart (one column for evidence that the wolf is a hero; the other column for evidence that the wolf is a scoundrel). After reviewing all the evidence, each group reaches a conclusion about Cuthbert.

T-chart

YES, Cuthbert is a hero	NO, Cuthbert is NOT a hero.

CONCLUSION: We think that Cuthbert is _____

♦ In the larger group, have students share the evidence that supports their conclusion. Record all the evidence on a large T-chart.

open-minded

◆ Ask students if anyone wants to change their assessment of Cuthbert's character. Discuss the tendency that some students may have to look at Cuthbert only as a scoundrel because of their feelings about the wolf in *Little Red Riding Hood*. Ask if students have ever seen only the good or the bad features of something and later came to see the other side.

◆ Assign student to make a final choice, using the following format.

Second thoughts about Cuthbert

❑ *I have changed my assessment of Cuthbert because . . .*

_____

_____

❑ *I have not changed my assessment of Cuthbert because . . .*

_____

_____

Evaluation

◆ Assess the small group discussions for students' ability to make a decision about Cuthbert's character based on information collected from the story. Assess whether or not students were open to evidence supporting both the hero and scoundrel perspectives.

Extension

◆ Encourage students to look at more than one side of things. Ask students to think of a favourite thing (e.g., an event, television program, toy) and find one undesirable feature, and to consider a least favoured thing and find one desirable feature.

References

It's So Nice To Have a Wolf Around the House by Henry Allard (Illustrated by James Marshall, Garden City, New York, 1977).

The discovery

Critical Challenge

Critical Question

Should Professor Jack share his discovery with the world?

Overview

In the story *Jack and the Meanstalk,* by Brian and Rebecca Wildsmith, Professor Jack discovers a way of dramatically increasing the size of plants. Students brainstorm possible consequences of this discovery and weigh the pros and cons before deciding whether or not Professor Jack's secret should be shared with the rest of the world.

Requisite Tools

Background knowledge	• details of *Jack and the Meanstalk* • applications and consequences of immense plant growth	
Criteria for judgment	• the weight of the advantages (pros) versus the weight of the disadvantages (cons)	
Critical thinking vocabulary	• pro and con	
Thinking strategies	• T-chart	
Habits of mind		

Suggested Activities

◆ Read to the class *Jack and the Meanstalk* up to the end of the fifth page beyond the title page. Stop at this point and ask "What are the possible consequences or uses of Professor Jack's discovery?"

details of the story

◆ In small groups ask students to use words and pictures to record at least four things that might happen as a result of this new way of making plants grow very large.

◆ Introduce students to the notion of "pro" and "con" by suggesting that a discovery may have advantages (or desirable outcomes) and may also have disadvantages (or undesirable outcomes). For example, cars help us to get around faster but they also cause pollution. Explain that outcomes which are desirable are called "Pro" (promoting or supportive of the idea) and outcomes which are undesirable are called "Con" (contrary or against the idea)—"helps us get around" is a pro and "causes pollution" is a con.

pro and con

◆ Introduce students to a strategy for keeping track of the pros and cons of an idea by presenting on poster paper a T-chart with the heading *pros* at the top of the left-hand side and *cons* at the top of the right-hand side. To reinforce the concepts draw a happy and a sad face next to the words.

T-chart

Pro	Con

◆ As a whole class, have students present their ideas one-by-one as to the possible consequences and uses of Professor Jack's discovery and suggest whether each idea should be placed under the pro or the con column. If students are unsure whether the consequence is a pro or con they should seek advice from the rest of the class. (Students should suggest the possible positive and negative outcomes of each use. For example, an application of Professor Jack's discovery could be to grow lawns. A pro of this application would be fuller, quicker grass; a con would be that it may require a lot more work to keep the lawn trim.) Invite students to add more ideas to the T-chart.

applications and consequences of the discovery

♦ When all the consequences (pros and cons of each application) have been recorded, students should return to their original groups to consider the critical question:

Should Professor Jack share his discovery with the world?

weight of pros and cons

Students are to decide unanimously as a group whether the pros—the possible advantages of the discovery—outweigh the cons—the possible disadvantages of the discovery.

♦ Finish reading *Jack and the Meanstalk* and ask students to use pictures or words to say whether or not Professor Jack should share his discovery with the world.

♦ Invite each group to share its conclusion and to explain the reasoning behind its decision.

Evaluation

♦ Assess the group discussion by noticing whether students actually consider the relative importance or weight of opposing consequences.

♦ To assess if students understand the notion of pro and con, ask each student to use pictures or words to record two pros and two cons for attending school.

Extension

♦ Use this format for structuring class deliberations around other issues that students are asked to consider.

References

Jack and the Meanstalk by Brian and Rebecca Wildsmith (Oxford University Press, Oxford, 1994).

Rumpelstiltskin
and the conditions for kindness

Critical Challenge

Critical Question

Was it right for Rumpelstiltskin to demand something from the miller's daughter?

Overview

Students consider when it is that they have a responsibility to help others in need and when they do not. They then view the film *Rumpelstiltskin*, listen to the story and decide if Rumpelstiltskin was right in demanding something from the miller's daughter in exchange for saving her life.

Requisite Tools

Background knowledge	• knowledge of the story *Rumpelstiltskin*

Criteria for judgment	• criteria for assisting others (e.g., a person in danger; a person in need; an unhappy person)

Critical thinking vocabulary

Thinking strategies	• T-chart
	• story map

Habits of mind	• independent-minded

Suggested Activities

◆ Ask students to consider when we have a responsibility to help someone else when we are free to choose whether or not we will help. Organize the information volunteered using a T-chart such as the one shown below. Have students suggest examples that fall within each category.

T-chart

Times when we have a responsibility to help others	Times when we may help others

◆ Based on the examples provided by students, have them summarize criteria for distinguishing when we have a responsibility to help someone (for example, when their personal safety is endangered or when we have promised). List the criteria on a sheet of poster paper: "We have a responsibility to help others when . . ."

criteria for assisting others

◆ Show students the film *Rumpelstiltskin.*

details of the story

◆ Invite students to create a story map to retell and internalize the story, and then listen to an oral reading of the story to confirm that they have correctly identified all the main events of the story. (Story maps are geographic diagrams of the events which take place in a story; the focus in this activity is on events which take place in significant locations. Some stories can be more appropriately diagrammed on a timeline; this activity stresses the sequence of significant story events.)

story map

◆ Organize students into small groups to discuss the critical question:

Was it right for Rumpelstiltskin to demand something from the miller's daughter?

Remind students of the criteria they came up with for deciding when we have a responsibility to help others.

◆ Each small group should present its views and supporting reasons to the whole class. Discuss the issue. Ask students individually to think about the discussion and write down their personal position on Rumpelstiltskin's demand. Encourage students to decide in their own minds what they believe is right. Encourage them to explain why they took their position.

independent-minded

Evaluation

◆ Assess small group responses for the ability to use criteria in deciding to assist others and in justifying their position on the rightness of Rumpelstiltskin demanding payment from the miller's daughter.

◆ Assess individual written responses by looking for independent-mindedness–whether it appears that students have made up their own minds, or simply adopted the position of one or more others.

Extension

◆ As a follow-up, invite students to consider other issues arising from the story:

• Is it ever right to break a promise?

• Was it right for the miller's daughter to break her promise to Rumpelstiltskin?

• Was the King a fair (or good) person?

• Was Rumpelstiltskin any better than the King? (They both demanded material things in return for her life.)

◆ As an extension, present students with the critical challenge *Right or wrong?*

Making a difference

Critical Challenge

Critical Question

What might you personally do to make a lasting contribution to someone else's life?

Overview

Students are invited to consider what they can do to make a lasting difference in someone else's life. Hopefully, students will increase awareness of their own good fortune and there are always others who are worse off. The inspiration for the challenge is the picture book *A Handful of Seeds*, by Monica Hughes, which tells of a girl in Latin America who helps a group of street kids. Also instructive is the novel *Wingman*, by Daniel Manus Pinkwater, about a family insulted by being made to feel to poor.

Requisite Tools

Background knowledge	• knowledge of people's needs and behaviour	
Criteria for judgment	• criteria for thoughtful action (e.g., action is meaningful to student, makes a lasting contribution, respects the dignity of the recipient)	
Critical thinking vocabulary	• compare and contrast	
Thinking strategies	• Venn diagram • table of criteria	
Habits of mind	• respectful of feelings of others	

Suggested Activities

◆ Read aloud *A Handful of Seeds*, by Monica Hughes, a story which tells of a girl in Latin America who helps a group of street kids. Ask for general comments or questions.

◆ Look to students for a definition of *compare* and *contrast*.

compare and contrast

◆ Using a Venn diagram (in small groups or as a whole class) have students make comparisons between Concepcion's life and their own. Discuss which of the differences are positive and which are negative.

Venn diagram

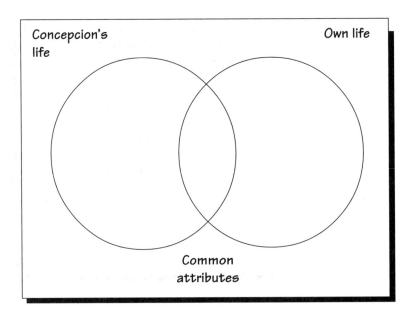

Concepcion's life   Own life

Common attributes

◆ Focus on the contribution that Concepcion made and talk about contributions that students have made to other peoples' lives. Discuss why a person might feel ashamed if he or she needed help. Relate this to a sense of dignity.

◆ It may be helpful to have previously read *Wingman*, by Daniel Manus Pinkwater, to the class, a story about a family that is ashamed at being given food because the gesture makes them feel poor.

respectful of others

◆ Put suggestions for people to help on the board and get students to add to the list: (e.g., a student who has broken his/her leg and is on crutches; an elderly person who lives alone).

◆ Ask students to consider the critical question:

> What might you personally do to make a lasting contribution to someone from the list?

◆ Invite students to suggest the criteria to consider in deciding what they might do to help someone else. If students do not provide them, suggest the following three criteria for these actions:

criteria for thoughtful action

- Action should make a lasting contribution to the other person

- Action should respect the dignity of the recipient

- Action should be meaningful to the student.

◆ As a class, brainstorm about actions that could be done. For each action, consider whether or not it meets each of three criteria. Use a table like the following to record how successfully the action meets the criteria that students have accepted.

table for criteria

Action	Lasting Contribution		Respects Dignity		Meaning-ful	
	Yes	No	Yes	No	Yes	No
#1 _____	❑	❑	❑	❑	❑	❑
#2 _____	❑	❑	❑	❑	❑	❑
#3 _____	❑	❑	❑	❑	❑	❑
#4 _____	❑	❑	❑	❑	❑	❑
#5 _____	❑	❑	❑	❑	❑	❑
#6 _____	❑	❑	❑	❑	❑	❑

◆ Have students in groups of three plan which actions they might undertake and why. Encourage students to implement their choice, but ensure that students understand that it is entirely up to them whether to do it or not. For each planned action ask them to explain why it meets the criteria.

Evaluation

◆ Assess student plans on the following:

- Do the proposed actions meet the criteria?

- Are students able to judge which actions met each of the criteria and which do not?

Extension

◆ As a follow up, share what students have done—for those who actually implemented their choice:

- What action did you do?

- How did you feel about your action?

- How did the person feel about your action?

- How could you determine if your contribution has made an impact?

References

A Handful of Seeds by Monica Hughes (paintings by Luis Garay, Lister Publishers, Toronto, 1993).

Wingman by Daniel Manus Pinkwater (Dodd Mead, New York, 1975).

Right or wrong?

Critical Challenge

Critical Question

Is it ever right to do something wrong?

Overview

The stealing of a trumpet in E.B. White's novel *The Trumpet of the Swan* is used to focus discussion on when, if ever, it is justifiable to do something that is wrong. In this story the parent of a young swan steals a trumpet to provide the young voiceless swan with a way to communicate. Other stories which raise a similar dilemma may also be used—for example, "Robin Hood" (stealing from the rich to give to the poor) or "Jack and the Beanstalk" (stealing a hen to provide food).

Requisite Tools

Background knowledge	• knowledge of the consequences of various actions	
Criteria for judgment	• criteria of acceptable action (e.g., must cause less harm than it prevents, must be fair to everyone who may be affected)	
Critical thinking vocabulary		
Thinking strategies	• imagining the consequences in hypothetical situations	
Habits of mind		

Suggested Activities

◆ Read aloud *The Trumpet of the Swan* up to page 80. Ask students to describe what the swan did (i.e., steal the trumpet) and why. Ask students if they think what the swan did was justified or not?

◆ In small groups, have students discuss the critical question:

Is it ever right to do something wrong?

Students should draw upon the story and their own experiences to reach an answer. Depending on the discussions, it may be useful to provide a few hypothetical situations to spark students thinking (e.g., Would it be wrong to steal food from a rich person if my child was starving to death? Would it be wrong to steal a chocolate bar from store owner if I wanted to have a snack?)

imagining the consequences

◆ After their discussions, students must each provide their own answer to the critical challenge.

◆ Engage students' thinking by asking two questions about the fairness and consequences of their decisions:

• Put yourself in the position of the individuals who may be affected by the action. Would it be fair to treat them this way?

fairness and consequences

• Is the world a better place (are the consequences better) if the action is taken?

◆ Invite students to reconsider their original answer. Ask them to set down their answer and explain why they chose it.

Evaluation

◆ Assess student responses on the following basis: Do they consider fairness (not necessarily the word) and the consequences of the action?

Extension

◆ Finish reading the novel and draw attention to the young swan's efforts to "right the wrong"—to pay back for his father's theft. Discuss whether the swan had a responsibility to try to make up for the wrong. Have students discuss when in their own life they felt that they should make up for a wrong?

References

Trumpet of the Swan by E.B. White (illustrations by Edward Froscino, Harper and Row, New York, 1970).

My own character and personality traits

Critical Challenge

Critical Task

Identify three traits that reflect how others see you.

Overview

Students are asked to judge what kinds of character or personality traits are positive. Using that knowledge, students choose three positive traits which best fit themselves. Other students then try to guess which traits fit which students, and to provide evidence to support their guesses.

Requisite Tools

Background knowledge	• personal knowledge of themselves and others	
Criteria for judgment	• positive and negative personality traits • traits reflect how others see the person	
Critical thinking vocabulary	• point of view	
Thinking strategies	• Think-Pair-Share	
Habits of mind	• respect for others' views and feelings	

Suggested Activities

◆ Using a Think-Pair-Share strategy ask students to form pairs and brainstorm a list of words that describe positive, non-physical character or personality traits (e.g., funny, friendly, smart).

Think-Pair-Share

◆ Ask pairs to report back to the class the words they choose and compile a list of all the words on large paper or a blackboard. Discuss which words pick out which are positive traits and which negative. For example, is a word like "goofy" considered positive or negative? Why or why not?

positive and negative traits

◆ Ask students to choose three positive character traits that fit how they see themselves and record their choices on an index card.

knowledge of themselves

◆ Briefly discuss *point of view* —how the perceptions of others may not always fit our own perceptions. Depending on the students, it may be helpful to physically locate them in different positions and ask them to describe the differences resulting from the different physical locations. Ask if students can think of a situation in which they saw an event differently from someone else. Present the critical task:

point of view

> Identify three traits that reflect how others see you.

Explain that students should reconsider the three positive traits they've chosen and revise them if need be, so that they fit how they think others view them—their final choices should represent traits that they think others at school have observed. If students change their list have them cross out the ones they originally entered—but not erase them. Students should be prepared to explain their choices.

how others see person

◆ Collect the index cards and read the words aloud (one card at a time) to all the students. Ask students to guess which words fit which student. For each card, take three guesses from the class. Students who make guesses should be asked to explain, using evidence if possible, why the words on a card describe the person they identify. After three guesses, the student who chose the words identifies him/herself and explains why he or she chose those words. Remind students about not making comments that might hurt anyone's feelings.

respectful of others

Evaluation

◆ Assess students' understanding of the difference between a positive and negative characteristic label. Can students provide evidence for assigning a trait to a given student? In explaining a guess, assess how well students understand point of view—do they recognize that how others view them may be different from how they view themselves?

Extension

◆ Have students develop character profiles of fictional characters they have read about in their stories.

◆ Invite students to think of how they might influence people's perceptions of them. What could they do to earn additional positive character traits?

Powerful memories

Critical Challenge

Critical Question

Which of your memories is your most powerful one? Why is it most powerful?

Overview

The story *Wilfred Gordon McDonald Partridge,* by Mem Fox, explains how an elderly woman is aided in regaining her lost memory by a little boy who brings things that trigger her memory. This story is used to stimulate students into thinking of their most powerful memory and what makes it so powerful.

Requisite Tools

Background knowledge	• knowledge of memories and what they can be like	
Criteria for judgment	• criteria of most powerful memory (e.g., vivid, hardest to forget, effect on life)	
Critical thinking vocabulary		
Thinking strategies	• webbing of ideas	
Habits of mind		

Suggested Activities

◆ With the whole class, ask, "What are memories?" Invite students to volunteer some of their favourite memories and discuss what features memories can have (good/bad; powerful/frightening).

concept of 'memory'

◆ Read the story *Wilfred Gordon McDonald Partridge*. Discuss the different memories suggested in the book and classify them into categories such as happy, sad, funny, and scary. Create a web (or chart) on the board to illustrate the memories that might fit within each of the categories.

◆ Ask students to work individually to web some of their own memories under categories of their choosing. Then have them share their web with a partner. Share a few with the class as a whole.

webbing of ideas

◆ Suggest to students that they talk to their parents for additional memories to add to their web. On the following day, invite students to add to their memory web.

knowledge of memories

◆ Present the critical question:

> Which of your memories is your most powerful one? Why is it most powerful?

Offer suggestions about how students might recognize their most powerful memory: hardest to forget, has had the biggest effect on their life, or is the most vivid memory they have. Invite students to add to the list of criteria of their most powerful memory.

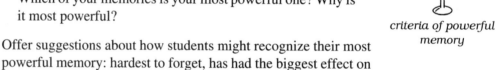

criteria of powerful memory

◆ Have sets of partners meet with each other and discuss their memories and the reasons they have for seeing the memory as their most powerful one.

◆ Ask students to identify their most powerful memory and illustrate it in a drawing.

◆ Students should then write about the memory, describing everything they can remember (e.g., the sequence of events, how they felt), and explain why they think it is their most powerful memory. Encourage students to work with a partner, asking each other questions so they can add more detail to their writing.

◆ Ask students to share their picture of and writing about their most powerful memory with the rest of the class.

Evaluation

◆ Assess student work on the appropriateness of the drawing, the written description, and their ability to explain in light of the criteria why they regard their choice as their most powerful memory.

Extension

◆ Ask a follow-up, assign students to work with a partner to discuss three questions:

- How do memories affect how we act?

- How do memories help us learn new things?

- How can we help ourselves remember important things?

◆ Ask students to write their individual responses to these questions in their learning logs.

References

Wilfred Gordon McDonald Partridge by Mem Fox (Puffin Books, Harmondsonworth, England, 1987).

Assigning household tasks

Critical Challenge

Critical Question

How should household jobs best be shared among family members?

Overview

Students imagine they are parents. They are asked to divide up four household chores in their own homes in a fair and effective manner.

Requisite Tools

Background knowledge	• knowledge of household tasks • knowledge of the talents of family members	
Criteria for judgment	• fair and effective division of tasks	
Critical thinking vocabulary		
Thinking strategies		
Habits of mind	• fair-minded	

Suggested Activities

◆ As a class, brainstorm the various jobs required to maintain a home. Make a list of the jobs on large paper or on the blackboard.

knowledge of household tasks

◆ Explain to students that they are about to decide how household tasks should be shared among members of their family. As a group, set criteria for determining how these choices should be made. Considerations should highlight a fair and effective division of labour among family members.

fair and effective division of labour

◆ Provide each student with a large sheet of paper and colored pencils. Ask students to fold the paper twice to make four sections. Students then imagine themselves as parents and make decisions about who should be responsible for four different household jobs. With drawings and words, students use the criteria to assign a household job to a family member including themselves and show the decision in one of the four boxes. Students should be ready to explain how their decisions reflect the criteria.

knowledge of family talents

◆ As a class, ask students to explain their job assignments and give reasons for their choices. Discuss students' choices as a class. Pay particular attention to the fairness of the tasks that students assigned themselves.

fair-minded

Evaluation

◆ Assess how well students are able to give clear and thoughtful reasons for their choices and whether or not their choices demonstrate an understanding of fairness and effectiveness. Determine if students are fair in deciding which tasks to assign themselves.

Extension

◆ Discuss different ways in which family and household decisions can be made. Who should make the decisions? What are the most fair and effective ways of making decisions in a home?

◆ Look at the roles of responsibilities of different people within a community. What needs to be done in a community? What are the most fair and effective ways of making decisions in a community?

The trouble with Mama

Critical Challenge

Critical Question

Is Monster Mama a good parent?

Overview

In the story *Monster Mama,* by Liz Rosenberg, Patrick Edward is a typical seven-year old, but his mother is a Monster. Students consider the question "What makes a good parent?" before reading the story. Students then decide if Patrick Edward's mother is a good parent and justify their answer based on criteria they generate and on evidence from the story.

Requisite Tools

Background knowledge	• knowledge of *Monster Mama*	
Criteria for judgment	• criteria of a good parent	
Critical thinking vocabulary	• evidence	
Thinking strategies		
Habits of mind		

Suggested Activities

◆ This challenge may be used on an occasion when students are talking about families or about parents. Invite the class to identify criteria for a good parent by asking "What makes a good parent?" Make a list of their answers.

criteria of a good parent

◆ Read aloud *Monster Mama.*

knowledge of the story

◆ Return to the list of criteria of a good parent. Ask students if they wish to change anything on the list as a result of hearing this story.

◆ In small groups, ask students to use the criteria, along with supporting evidence from the text, to decide the critical question:

evidence

  Is Monster Mama a good parent?

◆ Each group receives one piece of paper folded to form four sections. Referring to the criteria, ask students to draw a picture and write a sentence in each of the squares to illustrate or describe an incident in the story that supports their answer to the question.

◆ Have each group share their conclusion and use their pictures to support it. Ask students to indicate which criterion (or criteria) applies in each square.

Evaluation

◆ Evaluate the pictures in light of how well students used the criteria of a good parent when making their judgments. Can students provide evidence from the story to support their conclusion?

Extension

◆ Assess students in refining the criteria of a good parent, and in making use of them to judge other characters in stories that they read.

References

Monster Mama by Liz Rosenberg (illustrations by Stephen Gammell, Philomel Books, New York, 1993).

Powerful questions

Critical Challenge

Critical Task

Formulate a *powerful* question for a classroom guest.

Overview

In preparation for a visit by a classroom guest, students brainstorm criteria for a *powerful* question. In pairs, students use the criteria to assess questions they have generated individually. Each student selects a powerful question to ask of the guest.

Requisite Tools

Background knowledge	• knowledge of the guest speaker and the topic	
Criteria for judgment	• criteria for a powerful question (e.g., asks for a lot of infomation, open-ended, requires thought)	
Critical thinking vocabulary	• criteria	
Thinking strategies		
Habits of mind		

Suggested Activities

◆ Explain that a guest will be coming in the near future to talk about some topic that the class has been studying. Provide background about the guest and invite students to consider what they would like to learn from this guest: "What would be a really good question—a really *powerful* question—to ask?"

knowledge of the guest and topic

◆ If the class has not previously worked with the notion of "criteria" provide a definition (e.g., criteria are how we recognize whether something is what we say it is) and invite students to provide examples of criteria for familiar things (e.g., What does a nice person look like? do? sound like? What would a nasty person look like? do? sound like?).

criteria

◆ As a class, brainstorm criteria for the critical task:

What makes a *powerful* question?

Ask the class to select up to five criteria that they think are most important in recognizing a powerful question.

criteria for powerful questions

Criteria for powerful questions

* *give you lots of information*

* *are specific to the person or situation*

* *are open-ended—can't be answered by yes or no*

* *may be unexpected*

* *are usually not easy to answer*

This list of criteria was generated by a multi-aged class of K-3 students at Charles Dickens Annex in Vancouver, British Columbia.

◆ Ask students to think of one or two questions that they would like to ask of the guest. Encourage students to use the criteria in formulating their questions. Ask students to write out their question(s) or, if they are not able to do so, have a friend or the teacher do it for them.

◆ In pairs, students assess the quality of each others' question(s) using the criteria as a guide. Have students discuss how they could make their questions more powerful.

◆ Ask each student to write out the powerful question that they would like to ask of their guest. (Make it clear that students will NOT be required to ask their question if they do not wish to do so.) On the day of the visit by a guest, invite all students who so wish to ask the question they have prepared.

> ### Powerful questions asked of a World War II veteran
>
> - *Why did you fight in the war?*
>
> - *Do you remember some of your friends from the war?*
>
> - *Which countries did you fight over?*
>
> - *Where did you live during the war?*
>
> - *Were there any women in World War II? If so, what were their jobs?*
>
> - *What started the fighting?*
>
> - *Why was Canada involved?*
>
> - *What was your safe place?*
>
> These questions were generated using the criteria listed above by a multi-aged class of K-3 students at Charles Dickens Annex in Vancouver, British Columbia.

Evaluation

◆ Assess how well the first draft and final questions meet the criteria generated by the class.

◆ Assess students' understanding of the notion of criteria by asking each student to use pictures or words to record three criteria for a good pet.

Extension

◆ After the guest has left, ask students to consider which questions were the most powerful. Discuss these in light of the criteria generated by the class. Ask if students want to add to or revise their list of criteria of what makes a powerful question. Post the revised list in the classroom for future reference.

◆ Repeat this activity from time to time as other guests visit the class, or when students are framing questions that they would like to pursue when studying a topic.

Teaching the value of money

Critical Challenge

Critical Task

Design a learning centre or activity that demonstrates whether or not your classmates have met a specific curricular outcome related to money.

Overview

Students design an activity to determine whether or not other students have met a curricular outcome dealing with money—for example, that students can recognize the value of coins and give change for $1.00. The planned activity should meet criteria agreed to by the class.

Requisite Tools

Background knowledge	• knowledge of curricular outcomes related to money
	• knowledge of ways to learn and teach about money

Criteria for judgment	• criteria for a good learning activity (e.g., helps to learn, space and materials available, useful to all)

Critical thinking vocabulary

Thinking strategies

Habits of mind

Suggested Activities

◆ Read the story *Alexander Who Was Rich Last Sunday*, by Judith Viorest, to introduce the topic of money.

◆ Share with students the learning outcomes about money in the mathematics curriculum.

knowledge of curricular outcomes

Sample learning outcomes involving money

Kindergarten to 1

• recognize and name the value of pennies, nickels, and dimes

• use money as a form of exchange

• create equivalent sets of coins up to 10¢ in value

Grades 2 to 3

• identify and use coins and bills (to $100) to estimate, count, record collections, create equivalent sets, and make change up to $10)

• read and write both forms of money notation (89¢ and $0.89)

These learning outcomes are taken from *Mathematics K to 7: Integrated Resource Package 1995* (Ministry of Education, Province of British Columbia, p. 144).

◆ Form groups of three, and ask students to brainstorm about ways of demonstrating that other students had learned one of the outcomes. For example, can they think of activities which would show that students in the class knew the value of different coins and could give change for $1.00?

knowledge of ways to teach about money

Ways of teaching about money

• *hold a postcard sale*

• *have a garage sale*

• *hold a cookie sale*

• *collect money to donate to grizzly bear foundation*

• *set up play store*

• *set up a bank*

• *make up a play about money*

This list of ideas was generated by a multi-aged class of K-3 students at Charles Dickens Annex in Vancouver, British Columbia.

◆ Bring students together as a whole class to set the criteria for the activity or centre. Encourage students to think of the qualities that are required for a good learning activity.

> **Criteria for a money activity or centre**
>
> • *materials must be readily available*
>
> • *must have the necessary physical space*
>
> • *all children (ages 5-8) must be able to take part*
>
> • *students must have the necessary skills to take part*
>
> • *must take place during school hours*
>
> This list of criteria was generated by a multi-aged class of K-3 students at Charles Dickens Annex in Vancouver, British Columbia.

◆ Send students back to their small groups. Keeping in mind the criteria that were set, students must choose *one* activity to bring back to the class. Each group should be prepared to explain how its choice meets the agreed-upon criteria.

criteria for a good learning activity

◆ Each group shares its suggestion with the rest of the class. Students then vote for the activity that they think best meets the criteria.

Evaluation

◆ Assess students on the basis of how well their proposals required an understanding of the outcomes related to money and how well the learning activity reflected the agreed-upon criteria.

Extension

◆ Implement at least one of the proposed activities and invite students to assess the effectiveness of the activity.

◆ Ask students to develop ways to learn other things and to assess the learning.

References

Alexander Who Was Rich Last Sunday by Judith Viorest (illustrated by Ray Crey, Atheneum, New York, 1978).

64

Create a trick

Critical Challenge

Critical Task

Make a good magic trick.

Overview

Using some simple materials, students create magic tricks. The class discusses what makes a magic trick successful, including the idea of illusion.

Requisite Tools

Background knowledge	• exposure to successful magic tricks

Criteria for judgment	• illusion (and other student-generated criteria)

Critical thinking vocabulary	

Thinking strategies	

Habits of mind	• respect for high quality

Suggested Activities

◆ Prepare tables with a large variety of materials (e.g., dice, cards, straws, cord, cups, marbles). Ask students to guess what these might be used for. Invite students to tell of examples of magic tricks that they have seen.

knowledge of magic tricks

◆ Discuss with students what makes a good magic trick. Explain the concept of *illusion* —something that fools our eyes. If possible, show students a magic trick.

illusion

- Send students to investigate the tables and materials. Ask them to keep in mind how they could use the materials they find to make a good magic trick.

- Call students back and ask them to report on what they found and what ideas they have about using the materials to make good magic tricks. With the students set criteria (beyond the basic criteria of fooling people) for good magic tricks using the materials on the tables. Write the criteria on large paper or the blackboard. Possible criteria include: use of many types of material, size, or how easy the trick is to put together. Come to a final decision on three criteria in addition to illusion for good magic tricks made with the material on the tables.

student-generated criteria

- Present the critical task:

  Make a good magic trick.

  Ask students to divide into groups of four and design magic tricks using the materials on the tables, and keeping in mind the identified criteria.

respect for high quality

- After sufficient time to put together the tricks, have each group demonstrate the trick to the rest of the class and discuss, as a class, what works well and not so well in each trick. What is interesting about the trick? What can be improved?

Evaluation

- Assess whether or not the magic tricks are successful in creating illusion and whether or not students incorporated the other agreed-upon criteria in their tricks.

Extension

- Work to perfect the group magic tricks and present a magic show to another class. Add diversion (distracting people's attention away from a trick) as a criterion of a good magic trick.